T0011767

COVID-19

by Beth Bence Reinke

PEBBLE
a capstone imprint

Pebble Explore is published by Pebble, an imprint of Capstone.
1710 Roe Crest Drive
North Mankato, Minnesota 56003
www.capstonepub.com

Library of Congress Cataloging-in-Publication Data
Names: Bence Reinke, Beth, author.
Title: COVID-19 / by Beth Bence Reinke.
Description: North Mankato, Minnesota : Pebble, [2022] | Series:
  Health and my body | Includes bibliographical references and
  index. | Audience: Ages 5-8 | Audience: Grades K-1 | Summary:
  "The COVID-19 pandemic has affected all of us. Kids are bound
  to have plenty of questions about the disease. Expertly leveled text
  and vibrant photos will help kids learn to recognize the disease and
  help prevent the spread of the virus that causes it"— Provided by
  publisher.
Identifiers: LCCN 2021002457 (print) | LCCN 2021002458 (ebook) |
  ISBN 9781663908070 (hardcover) | ISBN 9781663921000
  (paperback) | ISBN 9781663908049 (pdf) | ISBN 9781663908063
  (kindle edition)
Subjects: LCSH: COVID-19 (Disease)—Juvenile literature. |
  COVID-19 (Disease)—Prevention—Juvenile literature. | COVID-19
  (Disease)—Miscellanea.
Classification: LCC RA644.C67 B46 2022 (print) | LCC RA644.C67
  (ebook) | DDC 614.5/92414—dc23
LC record available at https://lccn.loc.gov/2021002457
LC ebook record available at https://lccn.loc.gov/2021002458

Printed and bound in China. 4205

Table of Contents

Words in **bold** are in the glossary.

What Is COVID-19?

Many people have heard of COVID-19. But what is it? COVID-19 is a disease caused by a **virus**. A virus is a tiny germ that makes people sick. Viruses cause many diseases.

COVID-19 stands for **Coronavirus** Disease 2019. Coronaviruses are a group of viruses. Each coronavirus in the group has its own name. The coronavirus that causes COVID-19 is called SARS-CoV-2.

Anyone can get COVID-19.

All coronaviruses have spikes that look like a crown. That's how the virus got its name. Corona means crown in Latin.

There are many kinds of coronaviruses. Some kinds cause the common cold. The one that causes COVID-19 is a **novel** virus. That means it is new. Scientists and doctors are still studying the virus. They want to learn more about it. This helps us learn how to fight the virus.

A 3-D image of a coronavirus

The COVID-19 Pandemic

In 2020, COVID-19 spread to many people around the world. The World Health Organization (WHO) called it a **pandemic**.

There have been many pandemics in the past. The Black Death was a pandemic in the 1300s. The last pandemic was in 2009. It was called the H1N1 pandemic.

How the Coronavirus Spreads

The coronavirus spreads from person to person. There are three ways you can get it. It spreads through contact, droplets, and the air.

Droplets

Everyone exhales droplets when they breathe. Most people get the virus through droplets from an infected person.

Droplets come in many sizes. Larger ones can be seen. They can come from coughing or sneezing. The droplets go through the air fast. They land quickly. They can land on a person close by and spread the virus.

Smaller droplets stay in the air longer. An infected person breathes out small droplets. If another person is near, they can breathe in the droplets.

Contact

The virus can also spread through touch. You might shake hands with a sick person. Or you could touch something that has droplets on it. Then you rub your eye. Or you touch your lips. The virus gets in your body.

Airborne

Some droplets can be very small. They can stay in the air for hours. They can also travel long distances. This often happens in enclosed spaces. If you breathe in these droplets, you might get sick.

Preventing the Spread of COVID-19

There are ways to stay safe during a pandemic. Physical distancing can help. Stay at least 6 feet (2 meters) away from others. Wear face coverings in public. Face coverings keep droplets from reaching others.

There are other things we can do to stay healthy. Try not to touch your face. Don't rub your eyes or nose. Do not put your hands in your mouth. It is also important not to share drinks or food.

People wear face coverings in public during the COVID-19 pandemic.

Wash your hands often to stay healthy. Wash before you eat and after using the toilet. Wash your hands after sneezing or coughing. Use water and soap. Rub the soap in your palms. Make lots of suds. Scrub the tops of your hands. Clean between your fingers too. Don't forget your fingernails and wrists.

You should wash your hands for 20 seconds. Count to 20 slowly. Try singing the ABCs. Or sing the "Happy Birthday" song twice. Ask an adult to help you keep time, if needed.

Viruses Inside the Body

In the body, a virus attaches to a healthy cell. The virus takes over. It tells the cell to make copies of the virus. Soon, there are many virus copies in many cells. The infected cells make you sick.

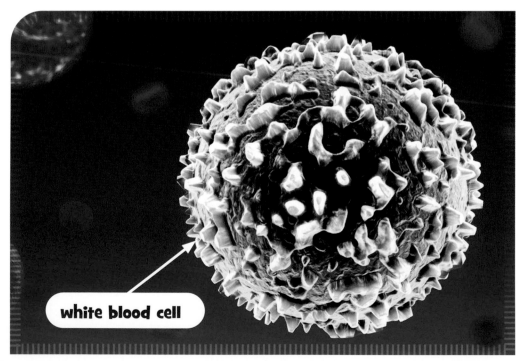

white blood cell

Your sick body responds. It makes **mucus**. It traps viruses. Mucus leaves the body through the nose or mouth. The sick person may sneeze or cough to get rid of mucus.

Your body also makes white blood cells. They fight the virus. Some eat viruses. Others make **antibodies**. Antibodies help get rid of viruses. You get better. The antibodies stay inside you. They protect you. If the virus comes back, antibodies fight it. They help you stay healthy.

Symptoms of COVID-19

COVID-19 has many **symptoms**. At first, a person may not know they have the virus. The first symptoms may show up in two days. But it can take up to two weeks for symptoms to show.

Many people with COVID-19 have a fever or chills. They may feel tired and achy. Some people may have stuffy noses. They cough. They may have a headache or sore throat. They may have problems breathing. Some people get an upset stomach. A loss of smell or taste can be a symptom too.

People of all ages can get COVID-19. Some people get very sick. Most are 65 or older. People who have other illnesses can get very sick with COVID-19 too.

People who are very sick go to the hospital. Doctors take care of them. Some people need medicines that help fight the virus. Others need oxygen to help them breathe. Treatments can help people get better.

Doctors give a sick person oxygen
to help him breathe.

Testing

COVID-19 symptoms can be a lot like symptoms of a cold or the flu. But an infected person might not have any symptoms at all. This makes it hard for people to know if they're sick. People can take a test to find out.

Tests are simple. For one test, a swab goes in the nose. It collects mucus. Another test collects saliva. Workers in a lab check the mucus or saliva for the virus. If the virus is there, the person has COVID-19.

If you do get sick with COVID-19, stay home. Cough into your elbow. Sneeze into your elbow, not your hand. Better yet, sneeze into a tissue. Then throw it away.

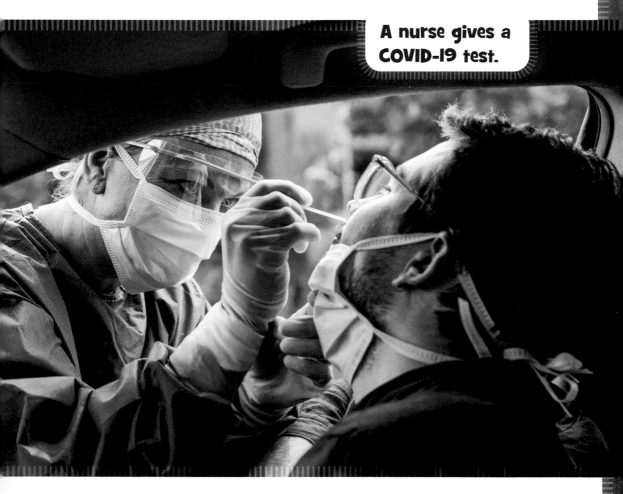

A nurse gives a COVID-19 test.

Staying Healthy

There are lots of ways to help your body fight off viruses. Eat healthy food. Fruits give you energy. Vegetables make your body strong.

Getting enough rest is important too. Kids need 10 hours of sleep every night. When you sleep, your body heals itself. Rest helps keep you well.

Exercise is also an important way to keep your body healthy. It makes your body strong. Be active for an hour each day. Pick a game and play hard!

Staying healthy means managing stress. Try not to worry about things. Instead, talk to your parents or a trusted adult. Talking can help you feel better.

It is also important to visit your doctor for regular checkups. Get your **vaccines**. They help protect you from many illnesses.

Kids exercise for good health.

Making a Vaccine

Scientists made a COVID-19 vaccine in 2020. They made sure the vaccine is safe. The vaccine helps protect your body from COVID-19. It helps make antibodies. Getting the vaccine will help protect those around you too.

To stay well, take good care of your body. You are in charge of your health.

Glossary

antibody (AN-tih-bah-dee)—a substance made by the body to fight germs

coronavirus (kuh-ROH-nuh-VY-rus)—a group of viruses that makes people sick

mucus (MYOO-kiss)—liquid made by cells inside the nose and breathing passages

novel (NAH-vul)—new and different

pandemic (pan-DEH-mik)—a disease outbreak that spreads across the world

saliva (suh-LY-vuh)—fluid that keeps the mouth moist

symptom (SIMP-tum)—a sign the body shows when it is sick

vaccine (vak-SEEN)—a substance that helps the body protect itself from a specific germ

virus (VY-rus)—a tiny germ that can make people sick

Read More

Biskup, Agnieszka. *Understanding Viruses with Max Axiom, Super Scientist: 4D an Augmented Reading Science Experience.* North Mankato, MN: Capstone Press, 2019.

Hustad, Douglas. *Understanding COVID-19.* Minneapolis: ABDO, 2020.

Levine, Sara. *Germs Up Close.* Minneapolis: Millbrook Press, 2021.

Internet Sites

Centers for Disease Control and Prevention: COVID-19
cdc.gov/coronavirus/2019-nCoV/index.html

Johns Hopkins Children's Center: COVID-19 Activity Book
hopkinsmedicine.org/johns-hopkins-childrens-center/patients-and-families/_documents/covid-19-resources-for-families/covid-19-activity-book.pdf

KidsHealth: Coronavirus: What Kids Can Do
kidshealth.org/en/kids/coronavirus-kids.html

Index